DOG BREEDS: DOG BREED PROFILES

Find Your Perfect Canine Companion

Faizal Ayotte

First Printing: 2015

ISBN-13:978-1519437907
ISBN-10:1519437900

Duel City Books

CONTENTS

COCKER SPANIEL

Cocker spaniels are among the most beautiful dogs thanks to their distinctive large, floppy ears and their graceful body. It is quite surprising that people used this seemingly homely breed as a hunting dog years ago. However, those days are long gone and the popularity of the cocker spaniel is largely attributable to its appeal as a family dog.

These delightful creatures are nice to have around children because they are smaller than most other breeds. It is rare to find a cocker spaniel taller than 16 inches at the shoulder. They are also quite light and rarely weigh more than 30lbs. Cocker spaniels have attractive dark eyes and light hair around the legs. Mostly found in tan, they also have cream, black, and even orange coats.

Cocker spaniels have experienced a rather difficult time in their history as companions for humans. For some time, breeders were reproducing spaniels with aggressive behavioral traits, which was possibly to increase their appeal as hunting dogs. However, due to its increasingly aggressive nature, people began to perceive the breed negatively over time.

Today, breeding the cocker spaniels is to have milder temperaments and characteristics that are more amiable. This has made the creatures extremely popular, especially with young children. They are also quite safe to have around other pets as the present breeds have all but lost their hunting traits. One of the most certain ways to get a mild-mannered cocker spaniel is to see a good breeder and see both the parents of the spaniel.

Cocker spaniels adjust easily to small houses and apartments since they are neither large nor do they require a lot of space or physical activity. Nonetheless, cocker spaniels do require regular exercise in order to maintain good health and a pleasant temper. They enjoy playing with children and owners can train them to perform tricks.

Training is a good way to ensure that your cocker spaniel continues to behave well. The training is not as important to make the cocker spaniel less of a threat around your children, but to learn more about your companion and to develop a positive friendship. Early training also helps your companion to adjust easily and comfortably to the environment of your home.

Although they are quite safe animals, cocker spaniels are difficult to maintain and you might spend a lot of time on their grooming and maintenance. Cocker spaniels' hair grow at a fast pace and require regular clipping and brushing is essential to maintain a neat and shiny coat. The big ears of the cocker spaniel provide a safe spot for dirt and grime to settle in; so make sure that you properly clean these areas every day.

You also need to pay a lot of attention to how you feed your cocker spaniel. Owner need to feed cocker spaniels at frequent intervals, so make sure that you prepare smaller portions to feed them several times throughout the day.

The portion sizes should be small and not contain many calories because cocker spaniels have a propensity to suffer from obesity and heart disease.

With its infectious charm and energy, the cocker spaniel can be the best friendly companion for you and your family.

A true working dog, the handsome Siberian Husky is synonymous with sleds and icy landscapes. Despite being a working dog, it is an excellent and loyal companion. Originally, the purpose of the breed was to pull sleds over long distances on icy terrain. Apart from that, they offer friendly company to their owners in the dreary cold months.

The American Kennel Club places the Siberian Husky in the working group. Being hard workers, the best way to keep this breed safe and in a good temperament is to keep them busy with work. One must note that these are not exactly house pets since they are genetically closer to wolves than other domesticated dog breeds. These large dogs reach a height of 20 to 24 inches and can weigh up to 60 lbs.

The Siberian Husky is a very energetic animal. It has a thick coat often in multiple colors of white, grey, or silver. The ears and face of the Siberian Husky closely resemble the wolf while the eyes are its most attractive feature.

Action-oriented animals, Siberian Huskies frequently get into trouble because of their impulsive nature. Their escapades often result in injuries; so be prepared to make quite a few trips to the veterinarian if you get yourself a Siberian Husky. Be extra vigilant during the first few days after getting your pet because they have a tendency to escape and run away.

Siberian Huskies love the outdoors and forcing them to stay indoors or in a small fenced yard is unfair. You will need to take them out into large open spaces so that they get their exercise and satisfy their wanderlust. Make sure that your house is well fenced because you don't want them to escape repeatedly.

When you keep a Siberian Husky, it is essential that you assert your dominance from the very first day. It is also important that you instantly enroll your pet in obedience training since it helps to get rid of difficult behavior. Once they learn that you are the boss, training them is not very difficult. Good initial training makes them responsive to the owner's commands and socializes them with people in their environment.

Siberian Huskies have big appetites; and once they are hungry, they can be quite undiscriminating and will forage at anything, including the furniture in your house. If you find that your Husky is losing its appetite, one reason might be a lack of exercise or spending too much time indoors.

You will have to brush the rich coat of your Husky at least once a week to keep it clean and shiny. Huskies shed a lot, so regular grooming means less hair to clean off from your furniture.

Generally, the Siberian Husky keeps good health apart from the injuries that come from being too adventurous. Some ailments they may suffer from include hip dysplasia and hypothyroidism.

If you like an active lifestyle and like a pet, that requires constant attention, then the Siberian Husky is the perfect companion for you.

COLLIE

Collies are among the larger dog breeds because they can grow to a height of 26 inches at the most and can weigh up to 80lbs. At the same time, collies make excellent family dogs and are comfortable staying indoors although they need large spaces.

Collies possess a unique protective instinct for which they have been useful as herding dogs for many years. Some collies tend to be nervous by nature and require frequent comforting and assurance from their owners.

They are strong animals as well as being notable for their beautiful bodies. They possess almond-shaped eyes and upright ears that indicate vigilance and watchfulness. Collies have a beautiful coat with warm hues, but the texture can vary from dog to dog. Normally, smoother coats are more difficult to maintain than coarser coats. Collies require less frequent brushing than other breeds, and those with rough coats may do well with even less. While brushing, take care to remove any tangles since collies have long hair. Also, be watchful of skin damage near the eyes, ears, face and on the legs.

Collies love company and they make great family dogs. They are capable of responding to affection and are equally at ease indoors and outdoors. If you choose to place your collie outdoors, you will find it to be a dedicated watchdog never letting an opportunity slip by to let you know about an intruder on the grounds.

When you bring a collie into your family, you can expect to be as attentive to it as a parent is. Collies tend to have a mind of their own and they frequently get into mischief when they are young. You can get them to behave well by providing behavior training. This will also help to keep them off the household furniture and reduce the problem of cleaning up dog hair that they shed frequently.

Health problems can be a frequent issue with collies, although most of their health problems are eye problems. They commonly experience progressive retinal atrophy, which unfortunately leads to blindness. However, most of the time, your collie is likely to get into fixes because of their own mischievous antics and nervous behavior. When driving with a collie, keep the windows raised because they have a habit of jumping out of open car windows.

Collies are voracious eaters and they gain appreciable weight in no time. Therefore, you need to be prepared to allocate a significant budget to dog food. In addition, you must provide many opportunities for exercise to your collie to help them burn away the excess calories; otherwise, they could gain a lot of weight and contract disease.

GOLDEN RETRIEVER

The golden retriever is an impressive looking breed with a muscular built and large frame. Golden retrievers typically reach a height of 24 inches at the shoulder and their weight can go up to 75lbs.

A distinctive feature of the golden retriever is its wide head, which is one of the reasons for which people regard the breed as one of the most intelligent dog breeds. Golden retrievers are prized-species for their beautiful tanned, gold-tinted coats, although some retrievers also sport coats with white spots. Such animals are not as sought after as the purely tanned retrievers.

Golden retrievers make excellent sport and work companions. People have been breeding them as work animals and for companionship for a long time. They thrive in jobs that require them to be vigilant and use their stamina. They are commonly useful as sniffer dogs or as rescue dogs.

Golden retrievers have bundles of energy and naturally become restless if they do not have much space to move around or enough activity to keep them occupied. Give them a large area to exercise their strong muscles and you will have a contended canine.

Golden retrievers can be a bit troublesome at times especially if one forces them to stay within small-enclosed spaces all the time. If you keep your golden retriever shut up inside the house all the time, they can become very unmanageable when you do let them out.

Golden retrievers have a healthy appetite that helps them to maintain their strength and high energy levels. Make sure you are prepared to bear the expenses of dog food before getting a golden retriever. Sometimes, a retriever may need specially prepared food, so consulting the veterinarian may be a good idea.

Another thing that you need to be careful about is having a golden retriever in a house with small children. While golden retrievers are friendly towards children and can spend hours playing with them, they can inadvertently knock over small children.

A good idea is to have your retriever undergo obedience training. The younger they are the better it is to train them since older and bigger dogs are difficult to manage and discipline. With the required training, your golden retriever will adjust to being around small children. Obedience training also helps golden retrievers to socialize with other dogs and to keep their aggressive tendencies in check.

You will also need to spend considerable time grooming your golden retriever. They have long hair that becomes 'matted' easily, especially behind the ears. It is also common for golden retrievers to shed a lot of hair, which means that you will need to remove the hair regularly from your furniture and carpet as well. Regular brushing is essential to prevent matting and to control the amount of shedding.

Gold retrievers are also likely to get fleas and ticks from spending time outdoors, so make sure you keep watch for signs of such infestation.

Labrador Retrievers are among the friendlier dog breeds and can be a delight to have around once you are able to ignore their willful tendencies. However, it is not always easy to manage these energetic and frolicsome creatures because they are highly energetic and need a lot of physical activity. Make sure that you are fully prepared to assume the responsibility to keep them safe and well cared.

The Labrador retriever is a strong and reliable creature. They can grow up to 24 inches tall and typically weigh between 60 and 80lbs. Labrador retrievers have a lot of stamina and energy, which makes them excellent work companions. For their size and strength, Labrador retrievers betray a gentle and unassuming appearance. They have warm, brown eyes and coats in warm hues of brown, gold, or black. Interestingly, Labrador retrievers have a waterproof coat, which makes them quite fond of the water.

People prefer having Labrador retrievers are sporting and hunting companions in the outdoors since they are among the few breeds that have enduring stamina and are fond of physical activity. Whether you plan a camping trip to the woods or a boating excursion on the lake, you can count on the Labrador retriever to be completely non-fussy and entirely sporting.

While they make great sporting companions, they require equal amounts of care and exercise during their growing stage. As a responsible owner, you need to provide them with a lot of space for physical activity. These large animals feel uncomfortable inside small apartments and therefore make sure you have a yard or similar space for these animals when getting one for your family. Regular walks are necessary with a Labrador retriever.

Labrador retrievers also have a hearty appetite and need lots of calories to maintain their activity and strength levels. Make sure the dog food you buy contains high levels of proteins and minerals to help the Labrador retriever develop strong bones and muscles. This will help your dog to grow into a sharp, active, and able sporting companion.

The trickiest part about having a Labrador retriever is that they might not always be comfortable around children. Their huge size makes them cause for concern especially around small children because these energetic and muscular creatures can easily knock them over while playing. It may be a better idea to wait until the children are a little older and can be safe around a Labrador retriever.

One of the first things that you need to do after bringing in a Labrador retriever into the household is to start obedience and behavior training. Labrador retrievers are quick learners but it is important that they start young. As they grow, it becomes difficult to control them and they can turn into quite stubborn creatures.

Caring for a Labrador retriever's appearance is relatively easy. Cleaning the coat is important to get rid of dirt and you can accomplish this thorough brushing the coat once a week. You also need to keep your Labrador retriever's nails clipped short to avoid skin damage and infection.

Having a Labrador retriever for a pet requires an accommodating and patient personality. However, the experience can be very rewarding. Despite being a bit headstrong and boisterous, Labrador retrievers are not very fussy and make warm and affectionate companions.

BOXER

If you have children and want a warm and friendly companion for them that will also protect your house, the boxer is an ideal choice. The name of this friendly breed describes their uncanny ability to box their opponents with their front legs in a fight.

Boxers first became popular in Europe because they were widely used by the police and military for their hunting abilities. Over time, people discovered their ability to be friendly companions. During the World War II, many American soldiers adopted Boxers during battles on the Continent. When the war ended, these soldiers brought their boxers over to the United States, which led to their popularity in American households.

Boxers are medium-sized dogs and they weigh up to 80lbs at the most. Despite this, they are string creatures and can even match the strength of some of the larger breeds. Known to have high levels of energy and muscle power, boxers can be fun to have. They have a distinctive wide chest and face. They are famous for having expressive and engaging eyes that can even melt the heart of most people.

Generally, the body of a boxer possesses fawn and tawny marks, while some boxers may even have additional black or white marks on their coat. While the black marks are an acceptable part of the boxer's coat, the white marks are a warning sign since they indicate existing or possible health problems for the boxer. Owners of Boxers with white marking cannot let their pets to take part in dog shows.

Due to their size and energy levels, boxers need regular exercise and a lot of space. If you live in an apartment or in a house that does not have open space, you should not consider getting a boxer. If you have a yard, make sure that you raise a higher fence because boxers can easily jump over shorter fences.

Boxers have an aggressive personality streak at times, so if you have other smaller pets in the house, it may not be a good idea to get a boxer. Boxers can be aggressive and bullying towards other pets in the house. It may help if you get a neutered boxer.

As far as children are concerned, boxers are friendly towards them but you may want to wait until your children have grown a little before getting a boxer since they can easily knock over toddlers and small children.

One of the first things you need to do once you get a boxer is to get it enrolled in obedience classes. Boxers have huge amounts of energy that needs utilizing correctly; otherwise, they can become hard to control. Boxer puppies need help with learning manners and getting along with other dogs. Boxers are intelligent animals and they learn to obey basic commands in very little time. They are affectionate and respond well to praise and acknowledgement.

Grooming for your boxer requires little effort. You need to brush their coat once a week. Other than that, you may need to clip the boxer's nails to avoid tears and infection. Since boxers are voracious eaters, they also need their teeth brushed regularly.

Common health problems associated with boxers are overeating, hip dysplasia, and heart disease. Feeding a specially formulated diet and getting a thyroid diagnosis of your boxer is important in order to maintain the health of your companion.

With their friendly nature and unending energy levels, boxers make amazing pets for any household.

BULLDOG

Bulldogs are very affectionate creatures and people feel particularly drawn to them due to their warm eyes. The distinguishing features of bulldogs are their sad-looking eyes and heavy jaws. In reality, bulldogs can be mild-mannered and gentle companions.

Bulldogs have a bit of history. Initially, breeding these creatures was as bull baiters and they had a more aggressive personality than the bulldogs of today. Once the popularity of bull baiting declined, however, breeders began developing more amiable and gentle breeds of bulldogs. The bulldogs we find today are extremely gentle and friendly compared to their ancestors.

Bulldogs retain their strength even today. They are not as large as Alsatians are, but they can reach heights of 16 inches and can weigh up to 50lbs. They have a thick body with heavyset jaws. A pair of dark eyes is set within a flat face.

Bulldogs are not sporting dogs because they are not physically active animals. Nevertheless, they make excellent companions and they are prized possessions as warm and loyal pets for the family. This characteristic of the bulldog makes it an excellent companion for people living in small houses or apartments since these creatures do not demand a lot of space.

However, it is necessary to give them some exercise during the day. A short walk around the block may be all the exercise they need in a day.

You need to be attentive to the health and hygiene of your bulldog. Bulldogs are prone to overeating, which can cause health problems like obesity, hip dysplasia, allergies, and breathing problems. Make sure you maintain a strict feeding routine to prevent overfeeding your bulldog. Bulldogs also have fragile windpipes.

Instead of making them wear a collar, it is better that you get a harness for your bulldog for walking them around. Bulldogs need protection from the sun. Keeping them out in the heat unprotected can result in overheating of their body, which can be dangerous for them.

Bulldogs also have a tendency to drool and pass air. Sometimes, they can get aggressive towards other dogs in competition for food. Keeping your bulldog clean is a big responsibility. Because of their thick skin and the numerous folds and wrinkles, it is necessary to groom and clean your bulldog daily to avoid infestations and infections of any kind.

This kind of cleaning is also important because bulldogs tend to develop a bad smell if left without grooming for long. Since they have shorthaired coats, you do not need to spend a lot of time grooming their coats.

Training is essential for bulldogs early on in their lives. They are intelligent creatures and learn fast. Moreover, they love to please their owners so they learn better if rewarded for their effort.

Bulldogs are charming and affectionate creatures. If you can take out the time to care for them every day, they will make excellent and warm companions.

BASSET HOUND

It is nearly impossible to resist the warm and inviting gaze of the Basset Hound's large and evocative eyes. This, along with the genuinely warm personality of these creatures, makes them a winning choice for household pets.

Basset Hounds are widely regarded for their sharp sense of smell, which makes then a member of the hound dogs, according to the American Kennel Club. In fact, Basset Hounds can be so attentive to the smells in their environment that they may even become oblivious to any commands you may be giving them.

Basset Hounds have a distinctive appearance, their most noticeable feature being their large floppy eyes, which can reach as low as the ground even when these dogs are standing upright on their hind legs. These are not very large dogs and do not exceed 20 inches in height or 60lbs in weight.

They have short legs and a broad chest, which gives them an anomalous look. Despite a slightly awkward appearance, Basset Hounds are actually quite nimble and can fit into constricted spaces when tracking scents. Most Basset Hounds have black and brown patches on a white coat but other colors are quite common.

These creatures make excellent household pets; however, they have a tendency to make plangent sounds, which can be distressing for your neighbors. Basset Hounds are not too keen on exercise, but they still need it. A fenced yard can be a good place for the Basset Hound to play in, but you still need to take it out regularly for a walk to keep it in good health.

Basset Hounds have a friendly disposition and can get along fairly well with other pets and children. They are fond of pleasing the people around them and are quite amiable. They make excellent play companions for young children since they are not fussy and enjoy the attention that children are likely to shower on them.

At the same time, Basset Hounds are intelligent and can display independence at times. Do not be surprised if they do not respond to your commands. In reality, all they want to do is some unguided play with you. If you want to train your pet, make sure you do it while they are young and malleable. You can get your Basset Hound enrolled in obedience classes where they will learn to obey commands and to get along with other dogs.

One thing you need to pay attention to is the diet of your Basset Hound. These creatures have huge appetites and can easily gain a lot of weight, especially if they do not get enough exercise. A vegetarian diet prepared in consultation with a veterinarian can be a good way to help your Basset Hound lose weight and stay in shape.

As far as grooming is concerned, you need to pay extra attention to the area around the ears. These places are likely to be the site of infections and a site where dirt tends to accumulate. Make sure you brush the coat of your Basset Hound once a week and take it to the vet as soon as you detect difficulties in hearing.

Because of their unquenchable desire to get along with humans and please their owners, Basset Hounds are extremely congenial and loyal pets.

German Shepherds have the best reputations among dog lovers. Many regard these as highly intelligent, courageous, and strong. They stand tall at 26 inches and can weigh up to 75lbs.

They are alert animals with upright ears and watchful eyes. It is for this reason that they are widely used as police dogs and rescue dogs. Many people prefer the German Shepherds to the related Alsatian breed for the very reason that the German Shepherds has a more versatile personality and stable temperament.

Many people admire German Shepherds for their sharp protective instincts. German Shepherds are very protective about their owners and their territory, which makes them ideal guard dogs. However, it is not rare to come across a German shepherd with a neurotic personality. It is advisable to keep a distance from such creatures and opt for one with a more stable personality.

German Shepherds make excellent companions in addition to being great guard dogs. They are friendly and despite their size and appearance, are fond of children and other pets in the household.

Owners of German Shepherds must be prepared to spend a lot of time helping their dogs get the right amount of exercise they need. The large size of the German Shepherds makes it an impractical choice for an apartment or small house.

Along with physical exercise, owners of the German Shepherds need to engage them all the time. Unlike other family or ornamental breeds, the German Shepherds is highly active and needs to be engaged in some kind of work. They enjoy the company of humans and other animals since this offers them much opportunity to interact socially and productively.

If you are getting a German Shepherds puppy, make sure that it is not carrying diseases such as hip dysplasia or epilepsy. Once you have brought your German Shepherds puppy into the house, obedience training should be the first thing that it gets.

German Shepherds grow very fast, which makes it necessary to regulate their behavior and instincts as early as possible so that they can adjust to your house and follow the house rules without showing any behavioral problems.

You also need to ensure that the German Shepherds is social with other animals in your house or in the neighborhood. Behavioral training can be of great benefit to the dog in this regard. If you want to train your German Shepherds to be a guard dog, then make sure that you get a qualified and skilled trainer for the job. Usually, poorly skilled trainers end up making the German Shepherds excessively aggressive and even violent.

When feeding your German Shepherds make sure that the formulation contains a good amount of protein and other essential nutrients. Your dog may also require dog vitamins to supplement any deficiency in the regular diet, so consulting a veterinarian is very important. Grooming of German Shepherds is simple since their thick coat is not prone to matting. Brushing can be limited to once a week and nail clipping may not be necessary unless you live in the countryside.

German Shepherds make excellent companions due to their intelligence and loyalty.

It takes a special kind of personality to be the owner of a Chow Chow. Distinguished by their unique blue tongue, Chow Chows have adapted to being household pets from their origins as hunting dogs in China.

Chow Chows are prized species because of their appearance rather than their personality. They have rich double coats and curly tails. Chow Chows are available in a variety of colors including red, cream, and blue. The height of a typical Chow Chow is 20 inches and the normal weight is 50 to 70lbs. Classified as non-sporting dogs by the American Kennel Club, many people keep the Chow Chow as a household pet.

People tend to be cautious about the Chow Chow because of its aloof nature and slightly angry look. This leads people to assume that Chow Chows are not very interested in being around many people and do not need much petting.

Although originally people bred them as hunting dogs, the modern Chow Chows do not possess a lot of energy and can lead a comfortable life inside an apartment. Nonetheless, exercise is necessary for them to stay healthy. A fenced yard will provide the adequate space they need for daily exercise.

If you live in an apartment, then a walk around the block or in the park will do just fine. However, hold on tightly to your Chow Chow if there are other animals nearby because the presence of other animals around them can trigger their aggressive instincts.

Unlike their response to other animals, Chow Chows are friendly towards children and are affectionate towards their owners and their families. Getting obedience training at a young age is helpful in socializing Chow Chows to be comfortable around children.

Owners also need to work harder at asserting their dominance over the pets; otherwise, they can become difficult to manage. However, it is much more difficult to get Chow Chows to be friendly towards strangers.

The Chow Chow has a small appetite and does not require a heavy diet. When they are young, owners need to feed them with formulated puppy food. As they grow older, you can feed them regular dog food available in the stores. Grooming the Chow Chow is an area where you may need to pay more attention. Their double coat can be particularly difficult to brush and you may spend a lot of time giving them a thorough cleaning.

The thick coat of the Chow Chow makes it susceptible to overheating; so avoid having them out in the sun for too long, especially during the warmer months of the year. The Chow Chow may also suffer from hip dysplasia as well as pain in the knee joints.

The Chow Chow can be a good companion once it has becomes familiar with the environment and through proper socializing and training. While they may not be friendly towards visitors, Chow Chows will do well as personal companions.

The Chihuahua is an extremely popular breed largely because of its wide appeal among celebrities like Paris Hilton. An indulgent owner usually carries around it in its very own purse. The Chihuahua is naturally accustomed to warm climates and can therefore be sensitive to cold temperatures. However, many pet stores offer sweaters specially designed for Chihuahuas that can help them to stay warm when the weather becomes cooler.

The Chihuahua is an extremely small breed and barely reaches 5 inches in height and weighs 6 pounds at the most. The coat of the Chihuahua is usually tan; however, black coats as well as coats in other colors such as white and fawn are also common. Apart from color, there is considerable variety in the length of the hair. The alert set of eyes and large ears that stand on end distinguish this breed from others.

The American Kennel Group has classified the Chihuahua as a toy breed, because it mainly serves as a companion for its owner. Chihuahuas love to be engaged in some kind of activity with their owners all the time, which leads to a lot of pampering. Owners should never ignore a Chihuahua or leave it alone; otherwise, it can get very restless.

Chihuahuas live comfortably in apartments because of their small size. At the same time, they enjoy the outdoors and they will be quite at ease playing around in a fenced yard if one is available. They are also extremely easy to litter train. It is important to take the Chihuahua out for regular play and exercise, especially when the weather is warm.

One needs to be careful when leaving a Chihuahua in the company of small children. The Chihuahua can get a little aggressive around small children, especially if small children have abused it before, or if it feels the threat of rough handling. If the Chihuahua gets an overly indulgent owner, it is likely to become spoilt and dominating.

It is common for such animals to demonstrate aggressive behaviors, especially if their owners choose to ignore it. The Chihuahua is also a bit delusional as far as its strength is concerned and will frequently confront much bigger dogs and pets. This trait makes them somewhat useful as guard dogs. They are very protective about their owners and will immediately warn you about an intruder on your property.

In order to keep the self-centered tendencies of the Chihuahua in check, it is vital to get your pet enrolled in obedience classes while it is still a puppy. Timely obedience training and socialization will make the Chihuahua more responsive to you and will help it to get along better with children and other pets in the house. If they do not receive the recommended training, they can become extremely difficult and unmanageable. The Chihuahua also does well in agility training because of its high intelligence.

The Chihuahua is a fussy eater; so although you may not have to buy a lot of food, getting the specific food that your Chihuahua likes can add up to a big expense on your grocery bill. Usually, they prefer soft diet to a dry one. Some of the common health issues that the Chihuahua faces are fractures, epilepsy, rheumatism, and dislocated jaws.

If you have a Chihuahua with short hair, you may not need to brush its coat very often. For a Chihuahua with long hair, brushing once a week is sufficient. When you brush the teeth of your Chihuahua, make sure you do it thoroughly because they have very small jaws.

The Chihuahua is the perfect dog for someone who can resist the temptation to spoil it with too much pampering.

BEAGLE

Beagles are mild-mannered dogs and are widely used as hunting dogs due to their sharp sense of smell. Apart from this, they are a popular choice by many pet lovers as household pets.

Beagles have traditionally been in use as hunting dogs because they have an astounding ability to track scents and they can spend hours engaged in this activity. Beagles typically come in two varieties. The larger of these can attain a maximum height of 15 inches while the shorter variety only goes up to 13 inches at the most.

This is the only feature that distinguishes the two varieties as all beagles invariably have similar features including the characteristic droopy ears and dark eyes. The beagle has a shorthaired coat that occurs in shades of brown, black, and occasionally white markings.

Beagles are very energetic animals and they let out their energy in different ways, some of which can be troublesome.

Their incessant barking can invite complaints from neighbors, which makes them a poor choice for keeping in apartments. They also need a lot of exercise to stay fit, so taking them for a run in the park or a walk around the block is very important.

Although they are warm and friendly animals, beagles can be a bit temperamental. Be careful if you have other pets in the house, especially cats because beagles do not get along well with them. However, it is safe to have them around children and other dogs in the house. Beagles are also very sensitive creatures, so take care not to ignore or scold them, or even laugh at their antics. Once upset, beagles tend to sulk for days but they return to their usual self after that.

Beagles are intelligent animals and respond well to obedience training, especially when delivered in their early years. Usually, professional help is necessary because beagles tend to get distracted and may refuse to obey commands, especially during a chase.

One of the best things about beagles is that they are not fussy eaters. When they are hungry, they won't wait for you to dish out their favorite dog food; they'll simply make their way to the garbage can and find some scraps to eat.

If you want to keep your Beagle healthy, then regular grooming is necessary as it will take care of hair shedding and reduce the mess around the house. Beagles are physically active and this helps to prevent their nails from getting too long. Even then, you may need to trim their nails at least once every three to four weeks.

Beagles are hearty eaters and tend to overeat. You should be watchful for signs of obesity and take your beagle to the vet immediately to prevent further complications such as heart disease or epilepsy.

Overall, beagles are cheerful animals who adapt well to a household environment.

BOSTON TERRIER

The Boston terrier is a special breed for the very fact that it is one of the first varieties developed in the United States. Many people regard it as an integral part of the American culture.

The Boston Terrier developed during the early years of the nineteenth century. The American Kennel Club classifies the Boston Terrier as a non-sporting breed. In terms of size, the Boston terrier is among the smaller breeds with an average height ranging between 15 and 17 inches and a maximum weight of 25lbs.

Many people find the appearance of the Boston Terrier slightly comical thanks to its floppy jaws. Other than that, the Boston Terrier has a flat, square-shaped skull and a diminished muzzle. Boston Terriers typically sport coats in rich colors such as dark brown, brindle, and black. White markings spread across the body of the Boston Terrier. The shape of the tail may vary from straight to spiral.

Usually, the Boston Terrier has a white streak in between its eyes and on its chest. The rest of the markings are symmetrical along its body. These creatures have a pleasant demeanor and are easy to get along. It is extremely rare to find them acting hostile to visitors or even strangers.

They mingle comfortably with large families and are particularly fond of receiving treats. They are usually safe to have around children, but it is safer to have some form of supervision to check them if they get too rowdy.

Along with being very friendly creatures, Boston Terriers are highly energetic and intelligent. For this reason, they respond well to obedience classes and soon become manageable even in difficult situations. Because of their high energy levels, it is necessary to keep them occupied with some kind of activity or the other; otherwise, they get fidgety and restless.

Boston Terriers are very agile and flexible, which makes it easier for them to learn and perform a variety of tricks. Owners of Boston Terriers love to have their pets perform tricks before guests and in family get-togethers, and the Boston Terriers never fail at it.

Contrary to what many people believe, Boston Terriers can live quite comfortably in small houses and even in apartments. Having said that, it always helps to have some kind of open space for the Boston Terrier so that is can get the much-needed exercise. A yard with a secure fence usually does the job; otherwise, you can take your pet out for a walk in the park. It is important to maintain the exercise routine as breaks in the routine can make Boston Terriers irritable and edgy.

The Boston Terrier is susceptible to health issues related to the heart, sight and hearing. Cataracts and deafness are common ailments among older animals. They also tend to suffer from knee joint pain and hypothyroidism. This is the sad result of years of careless breeding of Boston Terriers with genetic defects. While diligent efforts have helped to bring the breed from the brink of extinction, it remains susceptible to disease.

Boston terriers also suffer from a weak immune system, particularly for the first six months of their life. One of the visible effects of the weakened immunity is the emergence of bald spots caused by a non-contagious demodectic mange disease. If the case becomes severe, it can also lead to baldness of the entire body. Sores also commonly develop in such cases. Treatment is possible through veterinary treatment and daily bathing and many dogs make a complete recovery. In some cases, however, infections persist and owners may have to put the dog to rest.

Boston Terriers do not have large appetites and maintain good health during their youth. Older dogs need taking out for regular exercise in order to avoid putting on weight. Older dogs usually build weight in the chest area. A diet formulated in consultation with a veterinarian can help to solve this problem. The Boston Terrier requires little grooming apart from the once-a-week brushing to keep the coat clean.

Boston Terriers can test your patience at times with their mischievous and noisy activities; at the same time, they are lovable and warm creatures, and they will give you wonderful companionship.

Photo " Bloodhound Trials Feb 2008 -2011" by John Lesli is licensed under CC BY 2.0

The Bloodhound is a popular and easily recognizable breed because of its portrayal in the movies as a convict-hounding dog. While the police mostly use the Bloodhound to track convicts on the loose, its keen sense of smell and ability to pick up scents also proves to be extremely useful in tracking down a lost person.

The American Kennel Club has classified the Bloodhound as a hound. It is one of the larger dog breeds. An adult Bloodhound can easily reach a height of 25 to 27 inches and can weigh between 80 and 110 lbs.

These dogs have a distinctive appearance and are easily identifiable through their large floppy ears and a wrinkled face. Despite their gloomy appearance, these dogs are very active and affectionate. The usual color of the animal's coat is tan or black with occasional red coats, which is not rare.

Contrary to the usual perception, the Bloodhound does not attack people, even when tracking down a criminal. They are useful as tracking dogs mainly because they are good at picking up and following scents.

However, if you plan to get one to guard your house, it won't be very useful. A lot of effort goes into training the Bloodhound to simply track down the convict and not leap to greet him once he has been located.

Despite being warm and affectionate creatures, Bloodhounds are not very obedient. Over the years, they have developed the tendency to be their own boss; therefore, obedience training does little benefit to them. You may have to get used to the stubborn nature of the Bloodhound for a peaceful co-existence.

A professional dog trainer can help your Bloodhound learn to follow a few essential commands. However, if you want to assume the responsibility for training your dog, remember to be patient at all times. Dealing harshly with your dog can have a negative effect on its psyche and will strain your relationship for good.

Bloodhounds need lots of exercise, so a fenced yard along with regular walks and runs in the park is essential. Generally, Bloodhounds fare better in the suburbs or in the countryside than in the city.

Food will make up a huge part of the cost of keeping a Bloodhound. These large animals have a hearty appetite and will frequently run up the dog food bill. Because this breed is susceptible to stomach issues, you should consult with a veterinarian to get a specially formulated diet for your pet.

When you groom your Bloodhound, make sure that you clean the skin between the wrinkles thoroughly. If left dirty, these spaces can be the site for bacterial growth and produce unpleasant odors. The floppy ears restrict air circulation around these areas, which can also give rise to infections of the ear.

Bloodhounds have a tendency to drool and slobber which can create a mess and require frequent cleaning. You may even have to take them to the vet for stomach problems and hip dysplasia.

The Bloodhound has an amicable personality and forms an unbreakable bond with its owner.

If you want a dog with a wonderful personality that's been able to withstand the test of time, then the bloodhound may be a perfect choice.

The Yorkshire terrier is one of the most popular small dog breeds because of its spunky personality and beautiful appearance. The Yorkshire Terrier has an amazing attitude and despite being a small dog, it is fearless and frequently takes on larger dogs in its environment without any fear. On the other hand, the Yorkshire Terrier is friendly and affectionate and makes a great companion for any owner.

The American Kennel Club has placed the Yorkshire Terrier in the Toy Group because of its small size. Generally, the smaller varieties are more adorable and breeders try to develop smaller and lighter varieties. The maximum weight of a Yorkshire Terrier is 7 lbs.

Animals weighing less than a pound are likely to be unhealthy and have short lifespans. The Yorkshire Terrier presents a delightful picture due to its long hair brushing against the ground as it walks. When getting a Yorkshire Terrier, it is important not to get an extremely small animal since smaller breeds would be unhealthy compared to the larger ones.

The color of the Yorkshire Terrier's coat varies from black to blue and silver while the rest of the body is of a tan shade. The tan and black combination is universal to all Yorkshire Terriers. Apart from the long, flowing hair, its sharp, dark eyes that peek out from the long hair dropping from its forehead also distinguish the Yorkshire Terrier.

Because of their small size, Yorkshire Terriers can live quite comfortably in apartments and small houses. Owners find it much easier to litter train Yorkshire Terriers than other dog breeds because they are extremely domesticated.

It is also possible for you to give your Yorkshire Terrier the required daily exercise indoors by playing fetching games within the house. However, it would definitely be healthier for your pet if you could take it out for a walk or run in the park.

Having a yard is also a good way to give your Yorkshire Terrier the required exercise without having to go further from the house. Simply make sure that the yard has proper enclosure with a secure fence in order to avoid your curious pet from sneaking out from any gaps or raisings in the fencing. Proper fencing will prevent the Yorkshire Terrier from getting lost while playing or, even worse, stolen by other children

Yorkshire Terriers are extremely sociable creatures and are comfortable in a vibrant family setting. You will find the Yorkshire Terrier an extremely willing playmate in various play and leisure activities with the family. They make excellent playmates for children, are generally quite permissive, and allow children to caress and play with them. Due to their small size and fragile bodies, however, it is not advisable to allow very young children to play with them. They could hurt the animal with excessive fondling and petting. Older children who are mindful of the sensitive nature of this dog can be trusted to have the Yorkshire Terrier as a friendly playmate.

Proper and early obedience training is essential if you want to avoid having to deal with a stubborn Yorkshire Terrier. Obedience and behavior training goes a long way to ensure that your Yorkshire Terrier is well behaved and properly socialized to your family environment. When trained properly by a professional, Yorkshire Terriers respond well to commands and can be safe from harm and danger.

Along with their small size, Yorkshire Terriers have an appetite to match. You won't have to worry about pet food bills a lot. However, when feeding a Yorkshire Terrier, do not restrict their diet to soft foods exclusively. This can prevent their teeth from developing strength, which can lead to dental problems later on.

Proceed from soft foods to regular dog food to help them develop stronger adult teeth. Along with dental problems, Yorkshire Terriers also tend to suffer hernias and hypoglycemia.

Frequent grooming is essential, and to keep their coat clean and shiny you will need to brush your Yorkshire Terrier at least thrice a week. Brushing their teeth regularly is also important to avoid dental problems.

As long as you take good care of your Yorkshire Terrier, you will find them to be the most amazing and positive companions.

Dalmatians have become a very popular breed since the release of the animated Disney film 101 Dalmatians. While Dalmatians are quite intelligent creatures and mischievous as puppies, there is more to them than what people continue to believe.

The American Kennel Club has classified the Dalmatian as a non-sporting breed, which can be surprising to those who mistake their slim body to be well suited to athletic pursuits. First, Dalmatians were useful to guard the coaches of noblemen in eighteenth century England. Later on, they were useful to pull wagons used by firefighters.

For many years, Dalmatians were most strongly associated with fire stations. Over the years, owners started to regard the Dalmatian as an intelligent, responsible, and hard-working breed.

Dalmatians are large dogs and can attain a maximum height of 24 inches. The average weight of an adult Dalmatian ranges from 45 to 65lbs. Despite being a slim dog, the Dalmatian is strong and muscular without being too bulky or hefty.

The most distinctive feature of the Dalmatian is its sleek white coat covered with brown or black spots. As most people who have watched the Disney classic will recall, Dalmatians are born without spots, but the spots appear later as they grow older. Apart from this, Dalmatians are also distinguished for having eyes that may be brown or blue, or even a combination of the two. The Dalmatian also supports a long and powerful talk.

The Dalmatian is an energetic creature and has a strong desire for companionship. Separation from their owners for a long period can cause them to become anxious and restless. They need a lot of open space to work out their high levels of energy.

Thus, if you plan to have a Dalmatian make sure you have a large yard and can take out the time to take your dog for a daily walk in the park. Dalmatians like to stay busy. You can use this to your advantage by training them to fetch the paper for you or other things in the house.

Despite being intelligent animals, Dalmatians are prone to being stubborn. Enroll them in obedience classes while they are young puppies; otherwise, it may become too difficult for you to deal with their stubbornness. Dalmatians are also shy and anxious by nature, so they need a good deal of socializing to become accustomed to the presence of other people around them.

Dalmatians require well-balanced, nutritious diet since they lead an active lifestyle. You may also need to feed vitamins and other supplements to your Dalmatian to make up for any deficiency in the regular pet food. Consult your veterinarian for good advice on specially formulated diets in this regard. Common medical problems associated with Dalmatians are deafness, kidney stones, hip dysplasia, and other allergies.

To groom your Dalmatian properly, you need to brush the coat once a week. This will help to remove loose hair and reduce the frequency of hair shedding.

A healthy and active Dalmatian will keep you on your toes at all times and be a perfect companion throughout the day.

ROTTWEILER

Rottweilers are intelligent and loyal dogs and owners have high esteem for them because of their commitment to protecting their owners. Versatility is an acknowledged characteristic of Rottweilers and people originally bred them as work dogs.

Appearances can be deceptive since many people assume the Rottweiler to be a docile lap dog; in reality, Rottweilers can be equally effective as guard dogs and owners can train them for agility.

Rottweilers are among the larger and muscular breeds. It can grow up to 27 inches tall and can weigh a maximum of 130lbs. The shiny coat of black or brown hair and evocative pair of brown eyes make Rottweilers a distinguished species.

Used widely as working or guard dogs, the Rottweiler has been the subject of unwarranted mistreatment. Sadly, owners have abused their Rottweilers to make them more aggressive as guard dogs. As a result, these creatures have acquired the notoriety of being dangerous and vicious animals. In reality, Rottweilers make warm and friendly pets if owners raise them with love and affection.

Since Rottweilers are large animals, they need a large area to move around and remain physically active. This makes them unsuitable for apartments and small houses. A larger house with a fenced yard is an ideal setting for the Rottweiler. They also benefit from a brisk walk or run in the park with their owners as it helps them to get rid of the excess energy.

Rottweilers are among the most intelligent breeds of dogs. Since they are excellent guard dogs, owners frequently assign them the job of keeping intruders and unwelcome animals out of the house and garden.

You must train your Rottweiler while it is still young, since these animals grow fast, and as adults, they can be too strong and powerful to be amenable to training. Along with obedience training, your Rottweiler will also need to socialize so that it can be comfortable around children and other animals. With some patience and love, the Rottweiler will become accustomed to obeying your commands easily. They are also highly active creatures, which increases the success rate of obedience and agility training.

It is necessary that if you have young children, you defer your decision to get a Rottweiler until your children have grown bigger. It is easy for Rottweilers to knock down or injure a small child because of their strength. Even supervision may not be an adequate protection against a Rottweiler knocking your toddler over accidentally.

Rottweilers are avid eaters, so you will be spending a large amount on buying dog food for your pet. As far as health issues are concerned, older Rottweilers tends to have joint problems especially if they you do not feed them with a proper diet earlier in their life. Making sure that you feed a nutritious diet to your Rottweiler is, therefore, very important.

Grooming a Rottweiler takes little time and effort. Rottweilers have shorthaired coats which requires little brushing. You may not need to brush your Rottweiler more than once a week as this will be sufficient to maintain a clean and shiny coat.

Although Rottweilers are quite active creatures, which wear down their nails sufficiently, you may need to trim them regularly if they get too long for their own safety and the safety of your family. Taking them to a vet regularly can help to keep diseases at bay.

Rottweilers are excellent companions because they help to protect your household and are affectionate creatures as well. They are warm and playful creatures and contrary to their reputation are not as vicious as they seem.

PUG

The Pug is an extremely endearing breed that captivates people's hearts with its warm expression and cute appearance. More than the appearance, it is the warmth and loving personality of the Pug that makes it a prized companion for their owners.

The American Kennel Club has designated the Pug in the Toy Group, which makes it suitable as a family dog. The Pug is a small to medium sized dog with a weight range of 14 to 18lbs. it has a muscular, stocky built with the distinctive flattened appearance of the face.

The face usually has a black coat covering it, often referred to as a mask. It also sports a curly tail that makes the Pug quite attractive to children. The coat of the Pug varies in color ranging from black to beige.

Pugs have a unique personality and their behavior varies according to the situation. Under normal circumstances, you can depend on your Pug to be relaxed, tame, and mild-mannered. However, upon the slightest indication of a threat to their owner or their house, the Pug can become aggressive against the intruder. As a family pet, Pugs are excellent and are safe to have around children. They have a very soft demeanor and will rarely act aggressively towards children in the household. However, compared to other types of dogs, Pugs tend to cause asthma are other allergies among children. Therefore, if your children suffer from these conditions, you must not get them a Pug.

Due to their tamed nature, you can maintain Pugs easily within an apartment. However, they are not lazy animals and take well to regular exercise. A walk around the block or a run in the park would do perfectly well to maintain them in good shape.

One thing that needs to be kept in mind that using a choke collar can block the airways of the Pug; hence, getting your Pug to wear a harness during the walk is a safer option.

While they have an endearingly affectionate nature, Pugs are slow learners. It can take a lot of time before the Pug learns to obey simple commands such as 'heel' or 'stay'.

Professional obedience classes can help largely, but the best reinforcement is the encouragement and praise from their owners. If your Pug does not show significant progress as a puppy, it would be better to wait until they have grown up a little and try again.

Pugs are not fussy eaters, because they love to eat. However, be careful what you feed them because you don't want your Pug to become overweight and suffer from knee problems in older age. Pugs are also prone to ailments such as Demodectic mange and eye injuries because of their flattened face. Make sure you take your Pug to a vet regularly to detect any early symptoms of these conditions and take effective steps.

Taking care of the grooming of your pug is very simple. Pugs don't have very long hair, so all that is required a good brushing of the coat once a week. That will remove any dirt and loose hair. Make sure you clean deep within the wrinkles to prevent bacterial growth and bad odors.

Pugs tend to snore. As long as you are comfortable with this, you will find them the perfect household pet.

Doberman Pinschers are among the few dog breeds that suffer from an image problem. Due to their negative portrayal in films as aggressive and ferocious creatures, Doberman Pinschers have acquired a poor reputation. The truth is that Doberman Pinschers make faithful and intelligent pets.

Classified as working dogs by the American Kennel Club, people initially bred the Doberman Pinschers for use as police dogs. They were too successful as police dogs and were later also inducted into the military. Their prevalence in these institutions has also contributed to the general fear of Doberman Pinschers among people.

The Doberman Pinscher has a characteristic conical head and a strong chest. It is a large dog and can attain a height of up to 28 inches weighing a maximum of 90 lbs.

Doberman Pinschers typically have short hair in varying colors of black, red, and fawn. Fawn markings occasionally dot the coat of the Doberman Pinscher. It is not rare to find a white spot on the chest of these magnificent creatures. Doberman Pinschers have dark, almond-shaped eyes. Many owners prefer to crop the tail of their Doberman Pinschers as it reduces the chances of injuries.

Dobermans are not widely known to be energetic animals. However, they have a lot of stamina and can work for long hours. These features make them less suitable for life in an apartment or in a small house with little open space. It is imperative that you have access to a securely fenced-in yard if you want to keep a Doberman in your house. Along with this, you will have to take your Doberman for a daily walk to help get rid of the excess energy and to bond with your companion.

Doberman Pinschers make great companions for children and are easy to handle. Watching a Doberman play with a child for a few minutes can be all that you need to break the myth of the Doberman as a ferocious animal. Doberman Pinschers are loyal to their owners and love to please them.

This makes them well suited to obedience training and socialization. If you plan to get a Doberman as a companion for your child, make sure you are there to supervise especially if the child is very small.

Socializing your Doberman will help you prevent difficult behavior with your pet. Without such socialization, Dobermans are likely to get into trouble because of their curious nature. Dobermans grow fast and can become difficult to train once they are older.

Due to their huge size, Dobermans enjoy a healthy appetite and need large quantities of food to maintain their energy and strength. You will have to make sure that the dog food you feed your Doberman is nutritious and contains the required nutrients for a large dog breed.

One problem with the Doberman is that it suffers from Von Willebrand's disease, a hereditary condition affecting the ability of the blood to clot after an injury. Another common health problem is hypothyroidism and heart complications. Older Doberman's become susceptible to weight issues. Most of these problems as avoidable, as long as you feed your Doberman specially formulated diet prepared in consultation with your veterinarian.

The Doberman Pinscher is a low-maintenance breed and does not demand a lot of grooming. Giving the coat a nice brushing once a week is sufficient. Additional care involves trimming the nails since long nails can result in injury and possibly infection.

Doberman Pinscher's are affectionate and warm creatures that enjoy being around people. They make perfect companions for children as well as grownups and do not mind a warm snuggle up every now and then.

The Miniature Pinscher is a perfect alternative if you want to keep a Doberman pinscher but cannot afford one because of its large size. The Miniature Pinscher has similar features and traits as the larger Doberman Pinscher but is only one-tenth of the size.

Despite their similarity, the two breeds are not closely related. The Miniature Pinscher is more directly relates to the German Pinscher and the American Kennel Club placed it in the toy breed group.

Weighing only 10 pounds at the most, the Miniature Pinscher does not grow beyond 12 inches in height. Don't be fooled by their diminutive size, however. Owners cannot treat these dogs as tame lap dogs. Like their ancestors, the Miniature Pinschers can be every bit the aggressive and protective dogs they were bred to be.

The Miniature Pinscher is a muscular and tough animal. It sports a black coat that may alternatively vary from deep brown to red and even rust in some varieties. The animal has a pair of deep brown eyes and a short-cropped tail. While some owners even like to have the ears of the Miniature Pinscher cropped, if left alone, the ears grow pricked up, much like the tail.

Miniature Pinschers have loads of energy, so even if they might fit comfortably in a small apartment, they need regular exercise in the outdoors. Be prepared to take your pet out for a daily walk to keep its spirits in moderation.

If you allow your Miniature Pinscher to play in a yard, be mindful of the fact that these creatures are curious by nature and will try to make their way out of the yard through any gap in the fencing. This can be dangerous especially if your house is near a busy street. Its small size also places the Miniature Pinscher at even greater risk of run over accidents by cars.

Although it is a small animal, the Miniature Pinscher is an aggressive creature. It can be irritable around small children and toddlers. You will have to restrain your pet if a stranger visits your house because it can become very aggressive towards them. If you have guests coming over and know that children will also accompany them, be sure to keep your Miniature Pinscher safely away from them.

Obedience classes are an absolute must because the Miniature Pinscher can be extremely stubborn and difficult to control. The earlier you enroll your Miniature Pinscher the better the chances of its learning to obey a large number of commands. In addition, you can also enroll your pet for agility training because they are highly active and are popular for winning competitions regularly.

These animals are also excellent hunters and they will keep the vermin population in check.

You need to be careful about the health of your Miniature Pinscher since they are liable to suffer from problems such as thyroid and heart problems, hip dysplasia and even epilepsy. These dogs also have a tendency to overeat and put on weight. Discussing the problem with a veterinarian can help as the vet could recommend a healthier diet for your dog.

The Miniature Pinscher does not require a lot of effort for grooming. Brushing once a week is good enough. You need to be more attentive to its nails and make sure that you clip them when they get too long.

Despite being a little hard to manage, the Miniature Pinscher is a very loyal breed.

Although this dog is not a first choice for everyone, you might want to consider this breed if you want a very loyal dog.

GREYHOUND

The American Kennel Club classifies greyhounds as hound dogs. These dogs have a remarkable ability for speed and are great breeds for competing in dog races. The Greyhound was a popular pet in ancient Egypt. It then gained popularity among British noblemen who started the practice of using these as racing dogs. The Greyhound then came to America where the practice continued.

The sad part is that once the animal gets old and begins to lose some races, the owners put them to rest. In addition to being excellent runners, Greyhounds make amazing and friendly pets.

Before you get yourself a Greyhound, ask a dog rescuer about the poor conditions in which some of these dogs may be. While it may be a great and noble idea to bring home an abandoned Greyhound, you need to know that these animals have developed strong prey instincts and may not be able to distinguish between what constitutes prey and what doesn't.

Therefore, you may not want to get one if you have other smaller pets in the house. Another thing you should note is that abandoned Greyhounds are most likely adults who have neither been potty-trained not groomed for obedience.

The Greyhound has a large and muscular body and despite its lean shape, it is very powerful. Along with a slender body, the Greyhound sports a part of dark arresting eyes and a long tail. There is no set color for the coat and it is quite variable.

Despite being such efficient racing dogs, Greyhounds can be incredibly calm and even lazy. It is not surprising to find them lazing around the house, which may be attributed to their being conditioned to save as much energy as possible for the races.

While it is important to have a nice big fenced yard to provide the space for your Greyhound to exercise, it can also learn to live in a smaller space as long as you take it out for regular walks. Because of their prey instincts, always remember to take your Greyhound out on a leash.

Greyhounds love being around people and playing. They make perfect family companions on bustling family get-togethers or a quiet, cozy evening. They like to cuddle up to their owners and are quite affectionate creatures. They get along well with children and are sensitive to any sign of danger to their owners.

Greyhounds require a good-quality diet to maintain their high energy levels. Make sure they eat in moderation to prevent them from gaining weight. A good strategy is to serve them small portions throughout the day instead of large portions twice a day. Consulting with a veterinarian is a good idea before formulating their diet. The veterinarian may also advise you if your Greyhound requires additional dietary supplements or vitamins.

Greyhounds shed very little hair so grooming them is no problem. Brushing once a month is sufficient. Make sure you also clip their nails if they get too long.

Adjusting to life with a Greyhound requires patience because they have been through so much. Once you cross that bridge, it can lead to an enriching friendship.

SAINT BERNARD

The Saint Bernard is an old breed, originally bred by monks in the Swiss Alps to help rescue stranded travelers from the snow. The Saint Bernard is a huge dog with a pensive appearance befitting its role as a rescuer of humans from the cold and dark slopes of the Alps.

The American Kennel Club places the Saint Bernard in the group of work animals because of its role as a rescue animal.

The Saint Bernard is a large dog and can reach a maximum height of 28 inches. The Saint Bernard is among the heaviest dog breeds, because it can weigh up to 200lbs. While the original Saint Bernards had shorthaired coats, their rising popularity in England during the Victorian era encouraged breeders to develop varieties with longer hair. Soon, people developed even larger varieties of the breed to satisfy the growing demand.

The focus on breeding Saint Bernards for appearance has contributed to a growing neglect of their personality. Over the years, Saint Bernards have acquired a bit of a reputation as bad-tempered animals. When planning to get a Saint Bernard for your household, make sure that you assess the temper of its parents in order to avoid ending up with a bad-tempered dog.

It is not ideal to have children playing with a young Saint Bernard. When young, Saint Bernards tend to be clumsy and can accidentally knock over toddlers and small children. As they grow older, they become more stable and are a pleasure to have around children. They make good playmates for children and will also look over them and keep them out of harm's way.

Because of its huge size, you should consider getting a Saint Bernard only if you have adequate space for them to move. These large creatures need a proper fenced yard to run around. Their ideal home would be a rural farm where they can get lots of exercise and open space.

However, if you live in the city, make sure you have the proper facilities to give your dog the required exercise. Saint Bernards can be easily bored; so make sure they have something to do or play when they are alone.

Obedience classes are necessary for young Saint Bernards because they learn to obey commands and be comfortable around other people. Delaying the process can make it difficult for owners to manage the behavior of the Saint Bernard. With the correct training, Saint Bernards can become a loyal and affectionate part of the household.

Maintaining a Saint Bernard is a tall order in terms of the expenses involved. These creatures need a lot of energy and you can expect to spend a huge sum on their food. Hip dysplasia is a common problem with Saint Bernards while they grow older. To avoid this, you need to feed them a specially prepared formulated food when they are younger. Also, be attentive to signs of heart disease and tumors in your dog.

Despite their long hair, Saint Bernards do not need a lot of grooming. They are easy to maintain because their fine hairs do not matt or catch a lot of dirt. Thorough brushing once a week is all that is required to keep the coat clean and shiny.

Other than being very large, nothing else could be a trouble to the owner of a Saint Bernard. They are warm, loving, and endearing companions.

STANDARD POODLE

The Standard Poodle has a bit of a dubious reputation, which is due to its appearance and people's assumptions about its personality. Some people perceive it to be a shallow animal while others believe it to be a highly intelligent breed. The reality is that the Standard Poodle possesses a great deal of intelligence, and is an extremely friendly and likeable companion.

Breeding the Standard Poodle was initially to serve as a working dog and back in the day it would help hunters catch water birds for hours at end. To protect the dog from lengthy exposure to water, the breeders developed the Standard Poodle to have its characteristic thick coat of curly hair.

While the curly hair persists to this day, Standard Poodles have long ceased to serve as working dogs and people keep them mainly for companionship. The Standard Poodle is a medium-sized dog as it rarely goes higher than 15 inches and weighs between 45 and 70lbs.

Despite its delicate appearance, the Standard Poodle is a strong and muscular breed. It has arresting brown eyes and characteristic ears that fold near the head. The Standard Poodle is easy to distinguish from other breeds by its short and erect tail.

While black and white poodles are quite visible, the breed sports a variety of coats including gray, brown, cream, and blue among others. It is generally observed that the black variety have a more restrained personality while white poodles are more restless and fidgety in comparison.

The Standard Poodle has a congenial personality and gets along well with children and other pets. If you already have a dog and want to get another one, then the Standard Poodle is a good choice, as it will get along quite well with your existing dog.

The Standard Poodle is playful by nature and will be comfortable around children during their play. While your poodle may seem to form an antagonistic relationship with your cat, it is just its way of showing an interest in play.

While the Standard Poodle will not give much trouble in an apartment, you should ideally have a large open space such as a fenced-in yard where the Poodle can get its exercise. If that space is not available, a daily walk around the block or in the park is highly recommendable.

Obedience classes have a very good effect on the Standard Poodle mainly because it has a strong aptitude for learning and because it really wants to make its owners happy. Without obedience classes, the Standard Poodle may never learn to overcome its instinctive aloofness around strangers. Sometimes, the poodle struggles to learn new commands and can feel depressed. It is important that you give it a command that it is familiar with as this will motivate it and give it the confidence to learn new commands.

If your poodle succeeds at obedience classes, you may even have it enrolled in advanced obedience classes and agility training. With the right kind of encouragement, Standard Poodles have known to do well in dog shows and agility competitions.

Standard Poodles suffer from a number of health conditions including skin and kidney infections, hip dysplasia, Addison's disease, and even epilepsy. Since epilepsy is a genetic disease, you can reduce the chances of your poodle suffering from it by requesting the breeder to have the parent dogs screened for the disease.

If you buy a Standard Poodle, be prepared to spend at least an hour daily to groom your pet. In addition to brushing, you will have to cut the hair of your poodle to maintain that manicured look. If you cannot manage it on your own, then it is necessary to take your poodle to a grooming salon once every five to six weeks.

Standard Poodles can be a joy to have around because of their friendly and playful nature. If you take good care of their grooming, these intelligent creatures can become excellent companions.

BULL TERRIER

The Bull Terrier is one of those breeds that suffer from an unwarranted negative image. The reason for this is the history of this breed as a fighting dog and that it has retained some of its aggressive tendencies.

However, as long as it is well cared for, the Bull Terrier maintains a cheerful temperament and is not aggressive. Families that have a Bull Terrier suffer from no dearth of opportunities for amusement because of the silly antics of this creature.

Care is crucial; however, if the Bull Terrier you are getting is an adult and if it has a history of abuse by the owner, as it can be unpredictable around children.

Part of the terrier group according to the American Kennel Club, the coat of the Bull Terrier appears in all white or brindle. The brindle coat often has white markings. With a muscular and powerful built, the Bull Terrier can weigh up to 70lbs. it has a bullet-shaped head and a broad chest. While the breed is closely relates to the American Pit Bull Terrier, they are separate animals and must not be confused.

The Bull Terrier adapts well to life in an apartment, if it gets its daily requirement of exercise. If you have a fenced area outdoors where the terrier can run around and play, it will help it to burn off its energy. They have a tendency to escape, so make sure that your house has proper fencing. In addition, the Bull Terrier does not get along nicely with other pets.

Bull Terriers make great family pets and are friendly towards children. They love to play with children and are particularly adept at catching Frisbees. While the Bull Terrier is comfortable around children it is familiar with, it needs supervision near unfamiliar children who may be visiting your house. A Bull Terrier may handle a small child or toddler roughly by mistaking it for an animal.

Bull Terriers need to know that you are an assertive owner. They are quick to sense a weak owner or an owner who is unsure and inexperienced. This can lead to the Bull Terrier trying to be the dominant one in the relationship and you will face a difficult time getting to control its behavior.

Bull Terriers can grow to be large animals. Thus, early obedience and behavior training is vital. The best time to do this is while the Bull Terrier is still a puppy. You can mold its behavior to make it more obedient and responsive to the owner's commands. It also helps your pet to become more socialized and comfortable in its new home.

Bull Terriers are happy eaters. They have a hearty appetite and run up a significant expenditure on pet food. When deciding the diet of your Bull Terrier, it is advisable to find out if it suffers from kidney issues. A veterinarian will recommend a specially formulated dog food for the Bull Terrier if it has a tendency to suffer from kidney problems.

Other than that, you also need to be alert to signs of hearing difficulties and heart trouble in your Bull Terrier.

In terms of grooming, you need to brush the coat once a week, because the Bull Terrier does not have very long hair, a thorough brushing once a week is more than enough to keep its coat clean and shiny. Also, make sure that you clean its teeth and clip its nails regularly.

A Bull Terrier will be a great companion for any experienced dog owner who has the patience to develop a functional relationship with his or her pet.

JACK RUSSELL TERRIER

Jack Russell Terriers are among the most energetic dog breeds. They have gained quite some popularity after the success of the children's television series Wishbone. Contrary to how the series depicted the Jack Russell Terrier, these creatures can be quite temperamental and difficult to manage.

Reverend Jack Russell initially bred the Jack Russell Terrier from where the breed derives its name. The breed developed in order to help chasing down foxes. The breed was small sized so that it could get into the small spaces and burrows where the foxes hid themselves.

The American Kennel Group has classified the Jack Russell Terrier as a terrier. Another related breed of the terrier is the British Jack Russell, which has shorter legs compared to the Jack Russell Terrier.

The Jack Russell Terrier is a small animal and rarely goes higher than 15 inches. The maximum that a Jack Russell Terrier can weigh is 17 lbs. Despite their small size, Jack

Russell Terriers are small animals. They look especially cute and endearing due to their bright, small eyes and constantly wagging, upright tail. Their coat is mostly white with patches of brown, black, or tan.

Keeping the Jack Russell Terrier in an apartment is not a good idea. These animals need a lot of activity to use up their energy and a small living space simply cannot provide enough stimuli. They are also likely to get into a lot of mischief because they prefer staying active until they have completely exhausted all of their energy.

In addition, they tend to have a mistaken sense of their actual size, which can cause them to end up in all kinds of scrapes and awkward situations. Therefore, a large yard with good fencing is the best way to keep them engaged and happy.

Jack Russell Terriers enjoy company and adjust well to life in an active family household. However, they have a strong need for attention, so it is recommendable that you acknowledge their presence from time to time and don't ignore them. Giving them simple retrieving tasks may be all that is needed to keep them happy.

A good way to control the energy levels of these creatures is to enroll them in obedience training. This will help them to obey commands and to socialize comfortably with other dogs.

Feeding and maintaining a Jack Russell Terrier is not a difficult task. These are low-maintenance creatures, which will not create a fuss over food or cleaning. Although they have high levels of energy, they have small appetites and you won't be running up a huge bill on pet food. If you note your Jack Russell Terrier showing signs of hyperactivity, you could consult with your veterinarian about a low-protein dog food.

This breed generally maintains good health; but you may need to be watchful of developing deafness and eye problems.

Because they don't have very long hair, Jack Russell Terriers don't require more than once-a-week brushing to maintain a smooth and shiny coat. If their nails grow too long, that requires clipping too.

If you can get used to their high energy levels and need for attention, a Jack Russell Terrier can provide you with hours of fun and joyous company.

NEWFOUNDLAND

Newfoundland dogs make the best companions for the family. The Newfoundland is a very large dog and has natural protective instincts which make them endearing. Despite their large size, the Newfoundland is a gentle creature and prefers to keep a low profile. However, they require a lot of care, so before getting one for your family make sure that you can invest the time in caring for it.

The Newfoundland is among the largest dog breeds and it is not rare to find dogs that reach heights of 28 inches. On average, an adult Newfoundland will weigh between 120 and 150lbs. A waterproof double coat of long hair protects the body of the Newfoundland. The common colors of the coat are black, brown, gray, and white. In some animals, the eyes may be dark brown while other animals may have lighter eyes.

Due to their size and protective instincts, the American Kennel Club categorizes Newfoundland dogs as working dogs. These animals serve as excellent rescue dogs and are in lighthouses where they play a crucial role in rescue operations in the water. Their waterproof coats makes it easier for them to move through the water and help save human lives.

Of course, a small apartment is hardly the perfect place for a Newfoundland to live comfortably. Although they are not very active animals and can are content with sitting by themselves, a fenced yard is necessary to help Newfoundland dogs get the exercise they need. However, they will gladly come along if you want to take them out for a walk in the evening.

Newfoundland dogs need early training to develop a pleasant disposition. Untrained puppies are easily excitable yet are instinctively cautious around young children. Obedience training can help them become more comfortable around the home and among strangers. Training a Newfoundland is a big challenge because their huge size makes it difficult to control them.

However, because they like to please their owners and they are social creatures by nature, they learn quickly. A well-acclimatized Newfoundland will get along well with children and other pets in the house without being too fussy or temperamental.

Because of its huge size, a Newfoundland has a hearty appetite. If you are considering getting a Newfoundland, you need to be aware of the amount you will be spending on dog food. It is important that you feed your Newfoundland food that is rich in protein so that your pet can develop strong bones to support its large body. Vitamin supplements may also be required and you must speak to a veterinarian about it.

Despite the luxuriant growth, grooming a Newfoundland's coat is not a difficult task. Brushing the coat once, a week is enough to prevent matting and remove dirt. You will also need to clip its nails once a month to prevent damage to your pet.

The Newfoundland is a friendly and devoted companion for the entire family. If you can take the time and effort to care for it, the Newfoundland will prove to be an unfailing friend.

BICHON FRISE

The Bichon Frise is an excellent choice if you are looking for a small and playful companion that does not cause any allergies.

The Bichon Frise is a small breed that reaches only 11 inches in height and weighs between 7 and 13 lbs. The Bichon Frise has a friendly and inviting appearance thanks to its beady eyes and fluffy white coat. The dog has a short tail that erects over the back. The American kennel Club has classified it as a non-sporting dog.

You may be concerned about having the Bichon Frise around small children because rough handling may injure it. Make sure that if you allow children to play with the dog, they are careful enough to handle it safely without causing it any harm or injury. If handled well, the Bichon Frise can be a good playmate for children of all ages.

Due to its small size, the Bichon Frise lives comfortably in apartments and small houses. It is a very homely animal and likes to be around people. However, every dog needs exercise, so having a fenced yard can provide the necessary space to play and walk around. Regular walks can help your pet to grow into a strong and fit animal.

The Bichon Frise has a malleable temper and is not headstrong by nature. Even then, basic obedience training can be very useful in socializing your pet to its environment. The Bichon Frise is playful and often lets itself out of the house or yard. Obedience training can help it come back to you when you call out to it.

Bichons are quick learners and are very intelligent. You can enroll your pet into agility training classes if you want it to perform tricks.

When feeding a Bichon Frise, you need to pay particular attention to the fact that feeding it soft foods regularly is likely to damage its teeth. A diet comprising of dry foods formulated in consultation with a veterinarian will help you to avoid dental problems with your Bichon. Make sure you regularly brush the Bichon's teeth to prevent cavities.

Be prepared to spend a lot of time grooming your Bichon Frise. Maintaining the pristine and fluffy white coat is not an easy task and your pet can easily end up looking like a dirty mop if you neglect its regular grooming. Make sure you brush the coat regularly. In addition to brushing, the coat of the Bichon Frise requires shaping and cutting every four weeks. Make sure you can afford what a professional groomer would charge for a grooming session.

Surprisingly, Bichons do not suffer from any major ailments and they usually have very good health. Moreover, they are highly affectionate creatures that are friendly and easy to control.

THANK YOU

If you have truly found value in our publication please take a minute and rate this book. We'd be eternally grateful if you left a review. We rely on reviews for our livelihood and it gives us great pleasure to see our work is appreciated.

28396958R00048

Printed in Great Britain
by Amazon